★ ★ ★

James Madison

James Madison

Brendan January

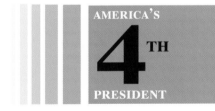

AMERICA'S
4TH
PRESIDENT

Children's Press®
A Division of Scholastic Inc.
New York / Toronto / London / Auckland / Sydney
Mexico City / New Delhi / Hong Kong
Danbury, Connecticut

Library of Congress Cataloging-in-Publication Data

January, Brendan, 1972-
     James Madison / by Brendan January.
         p. cm.—(Encyclopedia of presidents)
Summary: Recounts the story of America's fourth president, known as the
Father of the Constitution, describing his early life in Virginia and his many
years of service in public office.
Includes bibliographical references and index.
   ISBN 0-516-24210-5
   1. Madison, James, 1751-1836—Juvenile literature. 2. Presidents—United
States—Biography—Juvenile literature. [1. Madison, James, 1751-1836. 2.
Presidents.] I. Title. II. Series.
E342.J37 2003
973.5'1'092—dc21
[B]   2002011129

CHILDREN'S PRESS and associated logos are trademarks and or registered
trademarks of Scholastic Library Publishing. SCHOLASTIC and associated
logos are trademarks and or registered trademarks of Scholastic Inc.
1 2 3 4 5 6 7 8 9 10 R 12 11 10 09 08 07 06 05 04 03

Contents

Chapter 1

The Great Little Madison

James Madison, the fourth president of the United States, was called "the great little Madison." The phrase fit perfectly.

Madison was under five feet six inches tall and weighed about 140 pounds. He was described as pale and shy. During receptions in the White House, Madison wore a dark suit and seemed to blend into the crowd while his lively wife Dolley held the center of attention.

Yet Madison was a giant in American history. He didn't lead soldiers into battle or move crowds with powerful speeches. Rather, Madison used his pen. Long before he became president, Madison drafted a plan for a new U.S. Constitution, argued for it, and saw most of it adopted. He helped persuade others to *ratify*, or approve, the Constitution. Years later, he served as the fourth president elected under its new plan of government. After more than 200 years, the Constitution is still the framework for the U.S. government.

As president, Madison led the nation into the War of 1812. The conflict was filled with crises and defeats—British troops captured Washington, D.C., and burned the Capitol and the Executive Mansion. Yet the United States withstood the British attacks, and emerged from the war stronger and more confident than ever, thanks in large part to "the great little Madison."

"Never have I seen so much mind in so little matter," an observer remarked.

Virginia Boyhood

Madison was born on March 16, 1751, in Virginia. There was no United States, and Virginia was a colony of Great Britain, one of thirteen colonies along the eastern coast of North America. The colonists considered themselves loyal citizens of Britain, and many were proud to swear allegiance to the British king.

Since the early 1600s, white settlers had steadily pushed American Indians west. Most of the settled land was divided into farms. The colonies' largest cities—Boston, Philadelphia, and New York—would be considered tiny today. Buildings were no taller than three stories, and a visitor could walk around the city limits in an afternoon.

James Madison grew up in Orange County in central Virginia as the first son of his father, James Madison, and his mother, Nelly Conway Madison. The

James Madison as a young man.

Madisons were the wealthiest family in the county, and they owned large farms known as plantations.

James and his family lived on the plantation called Montpelier. At the age of eleven, he attended school in a neighboring county, studying with the sons of other wealthy plantation owners. Taught by a Scottish university graduate, James studied Greek and Latin, French, philosophy and logic, math, and astronomy. By the time he turned 18, James decided to leave Virginia to attend the College of New Jersey, later known as Princeton University.

Slavery at Montpelier

Like most wealthy Virginians, James Madison's family owned slaves. The first slaves were brought to the Virginia colony in 1619, shortly after the colony was first settled. Madison's father, James Sr., inherited 29 slaves, among the most in Orange County. Most slaves did the heavy work of planting, cultivating, and harvesting the crops. Others served as craftsmen and household servants.

Slaves were the personal property of their master. They had no legal rights and could be sold to another owner at any time. They worked six days a week, starting in the early morning, which they called "can see," to late in the evening, or "can't see." The rest of the time—evenings and Sundays—were their own.

☆ ☆ ☆

School Days

Princeton was a small sleepy town in central New Jersey. To get there, James, two friends, and a black slave set off on horseback. They may have traveled east to Fredericksburg and then northeast through Annapolis and Baltimore in Maryland to Philadelphia. There they would cross the Delaware River into New Jersey and travel on to the college.

James had never been outside Virginia. The size of the country and the variety of the people must have startled the 18-year-old. Philadelphia was then the largest city in North America. Compared to anything James had seen, it was a center of wealth and sophistication. The tree-lined streets were laid out in an orderly grid. Most of the homes were built from red brick and trimmed with white. At the dock, in a forest of ship masts, workers loaded and unloaded goods.

James arrived at Princeton in midsummer. In September, he took and passed the college's entrance examinations in Latin, Greek, English, and math. The college president was John Witherspoon, a leader in the Presbyterian Church, which supported the college. Witherspoon was a great influence on James. From him, James would learn about the latest ideas from Europe—especially ideas about how a government should be run.

School days began with the pealing of a bell at 5 A.M., followed by a church service an hour later. At that time, Princeton University was housed in one

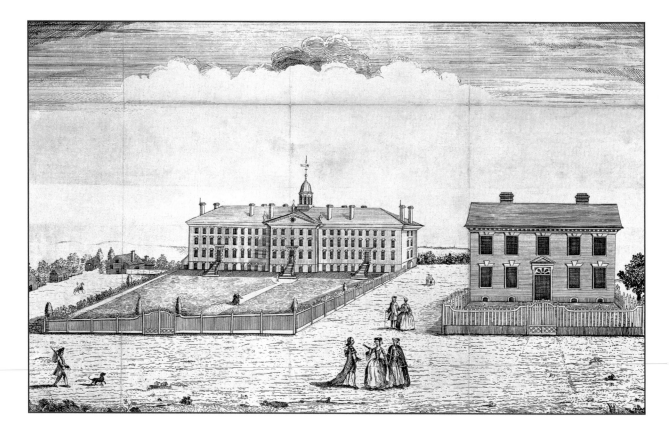

Nassau Hall (left) housed the College of New Jersey (now Princeton University) when Madison studied there. The building at the right is the president's house.

building called Nassau Hall. About 100 students lived and went to classes in the four-story stone building. James enjoyed his studies. He learned so quickly that he finished his required courses in two years instead of the usual three. Before returning to Virginia, he stayed at Princeton for a few extra months to pursue further study.

The late 1760s were exciting years. The British government imposed several taxes in the colonies, angering the colonists. In 1765, it announced the Stamp Act, requiring that all written or printed documents carry a stamp bought from the government. The stamps were to appear on books, newspapers, legal documents, and even playing cards. The British government reasoned that it had sent troops to North America to help defend the colonists during the French and Indian War (1754–63) and that colonies should help pay for their own defense in the future.

The colonists were furious about the new tax. They believed they should not be taxed unless they had a voice in the government. They refused to buy the stamps and organized demonstrations. "No taxation without representation!" they cried. Government agents who sold the stamps were threatened and sometimes driven out of town. Britain repealed the Stamp Act, but soon levied other new taxes on such items as tea and imported paper.

Many of Madison's classmates were swept up in patriotic fervor. To protest the British taxes, the colonists organized a *boycott* of British goods, agreeing not to buy any of the taxed goods. Some New York merchants decided to buy the goods anyway and sent a letter to Philadelphia merchants urging them to buy too. The letter was intercepted in Princeton before it reached Philadelphia. Madison wrote to his father that the letter was "burnt by the students of this place in the college yard, all of them appearing in black gowns and the bell tolling."

The Revolution Begins

After his extra months of study, Madison returned to Montpelier. He complained of his health and suffered from what he later described as "sudden attacks, somewhat resembling epilepsy." The farm routine seemed dull compared to his years in Princeton. He felt bored and out of touch.

"You are the only valuable friend I have in so public a place," Madison wrote to William Bradford, a college friend in Philadelphia. "[I] must rely on you for an account . . . of your part of the world."

A view of Montpelier where Madison grew up and where he later retired.

Madison began studying law books, and considered becoming a lawyer, but he found the books "dry and coarse" and soon gave up. He continued to follow the debates about the colonies and their disagreements with Britain. In 1773, a group of Boston patriots boarded British merchant ships in the harbor one night and emptied chests of taxed British tea into the water. Madison wrote to Bradford, "With regard to the tea, I wish Boston may conduct matters with as much discretion as they seem to do with boldness."

Soon, even the Virginians were preparing for war. As the son of a leading plantation owner, Madison was appointed a colonel in the Orange County militia. "We are very busy at present in raising men and procuring the necessaries for defending ourselves and our friends in case of sudden invasion," he wrote.

In April 1775, a British army marched into the Massachusetts countryside in search of hidden arms and gunpowder. They were met first in a town called Lexington, where colonial militia assembled. After a brisk exchange of musketry, the colonials fled and the British marched on to another town, Concord. By then, more colonials had assembled. Another battle began, and this time the British retreated, with the colonials sniping at them. The British reached Boston after an exhausting march, having suffered hundreds of casualties. The colonials formed a ring around Boston.

News of the battles spread through the colonies, reaching Madison at Montpelier. Everywhere, people spoke excitedly of the fighting. Some even began discussing independence from England.

Entrance into Politics

Madison was not well enough to serve as a soldier in the field, but there were other ways to help. In 1776, he was chosen to represent Orange County in a general convention to meet at Williamsburg, Virginia, to establish a new state government free of British control. There, in the stately brick homes and taverns of Williamsburg, Madison got to know the most powerful men in the state. George Mason, a leading figure in Virginia, drafted the new Constitution. Patrick Henry could persuade the assembly with his fiery speeches. Still only 25 years old, Madison usually listened more than he spoke.

Madison learned the most from Edmund Pendleton, who was the president of the assembly. Pendleton was not as wealthy as the other delegates, but he had great experience in law and politics. He also knew how to keep the assembly running smoothly. When delegates argued or threatened to walk out, Pendleton stepped in and settled disputes. He gently persuaded delegates to give up extreme positions and to find a middle course. From Pendleton, Madison learned a crucial element of republican government—compromise.

Patrick Henry addresses the Virginia House of Burgesses. His speeches there helped persuade Virginians to support war against Great Britain.

Madison did make one important contribution to the convention in the cause of religious freedom. Mason's new constitution stated that all people should have the right to worship as they pleased. Madison, however, believed that Mason's text did not go far enough. It sounded as if the assembly was giving people freedom of religion. Madison argued that the state had no such power—the right to freedom of religion was born within each individual and could never be given or taken away. With Pendleton's support, the assembly adopted Madison's small but important change in wording. It was his first contribution to American politics.

Madison returned to Montpelier in the summer of 1776, where he learned that the Continental Congress had signed a bold new document—the Declaration of Independence. The colonies, it stated, were no longer a part of Great Britain. Still, the war continued. British soldiers captured New York City and drove George Washington and the American army into New Jersey.

Madison returned to Williamsburg for the first session of the new Virginia legislature. Again, he usually observed and spoke little, but he did meet the brilliant Thomas Jefferson, who had written the Declaration of Independence. They served together on the Committee on Religion. The two discovered that they shared a passionate belief in religious freedom. It was the beginning of a long and close friendship between the two men.

In April 1777, Madison sought a seat in the Virginia House of Delegates. Most candidates encouraged voters (other male landowners) to vote for them by making promises and handing out gifts. Following the custom, Madison's opponent offered free drinks. Madison was disgusted by the practice and refused to do the same. To almost no one's surprise, he lost the election.

The Virginia delegates invited him to Williamsburg anyway. He was appointed in November 1777 to fill a vacant seat on the Council of State, which advised the Virginia governor, and took his seat in January 1778. As a member of the council, Madison learned an enormous amount. Along with its five other members, he considered and debated the important issues facing the Virginia government.

The American army, under George Washington, regularly sent desperate letters pleading for food, clothing, and weapons. As the war dragged on, however, these supplies grew scarce. Prices rose, and the paper money issued by the Continental Congress became virtually worthless. Worse, a British army landed in the southern colonies. Virginia became part of the battlefield.

Fast Facts

AMERICAN REVOLUTION

What: Also known as the War of Independence

When: 1776–1783

Who: Great Britain against the thirteen North American colonies, which were aided by France, the Netherlands, and Spain

Where: In the thirteen North American colonies and in the Atlantic Ocean

Why: British internal taxes and trade policies violated colonists' rights, so the colonists claimed their independence. The British found this unacceptable.

Outcome: U.S. and French armies accepted the surrender of a large British force at Yorktown, Virginia, in 1781, ending the major fighting. In the Treaty of Paris, signed in 1783, Britain recognized the independence of the American states, confirmed American fishing rights off Newfoundland, and ceded territory between the Appalachian Mountains and the Mississippi River. The United States agreed to try to end ill treatment of colonists who remained loyal to Britain by state and local governments and to restore property that had been taken from the loyalists during the war.

George Washington as a militia officer. When Madison became governor of Virginia, Washington was commander of the Continental Army.

Madison had seen government as a legislator. Now he saw it for the first time from a different perspective—from the governor's point of view. Madison learned that legislatures could be slow and very frustrating. When the governor tried to solve a problem or make a reform, some legislators disagreed, some asked for changes, some asked for favors or had to be flattered or threatened. Some might refuse to consider the issue at all. Only long, patient work and negotiation could accomplish change.

When he first arrived in Williamsburg, Madison was most interested in the theories that should guide a new republican government. Now he saw that there was a huge difference between planning a government and actually running one.

Onto the National Stage

Madison's service on the Council of State impressed many in Williamsburg. On December 14, 1779, Madison was one of four delegates chosen to represent Virginia at the Continental Congress in Philadelphia.

Madison was delighted with the appointment, but serving in Congress was a difficult job. The Congress was trying to coordinate the actions of all thirteen colonies in wartime, but it had very little real authority. The war was continuing, money was short, and inflation reduced the value of any funds that were available. The delegates argued bitterly with each other and waged furious battles against opponents in the newspapers.

For the first time, Madison, now 28 years old, could study problems that affected the entire nation. The delegates were trying to solve the problem of a *federal government*. How was power to be divided between the national Congress in Philadelphia and the individual states?

Two years earlier, in 1777, Congress had agreed on a plan of government called the Articles of Confederation, but the Articles had not yet been accepted by all the states. The main problem was a dispute about lands in the west. Some states, such as Virginia and Massachusetts, claimed land all the way to the Mississippi River. Maryland, a small state with no western claims, feared that if Virginia stretched all the way to the Mississippi, it would dominate its neighbors. Maryland demanded that the western lands be recognized as owned by the entire nation, not by individual states.

Thomas Jefferson—with help from Madison—helped arrange a compromise. He persuaded Virginia to give up its claims in the west. Instead, a western territory would be admitted as a new state when enough people had settled there. This action satisfied Maryland. On March 1, 1781, the Articles of Confederation went into effect.

In the meantime, the Articles were already proving to be too weak. Congress had no power to impose or collect taxes, and it had to rely on the states to contribute money. Yet the states were already raising their own militias to defend against British attacks. They could hardly afford to supply their own soldiers. They had no funds left over to send to Congress for the Continental Army.

A celebration in Philadelphia, where Madison lived in the 1780s when the Congress was in session.

Madison began to take positions of leadership in the Congress. He showed sound judgment and an attention to detail that impressed the other delegates. When Congress formed a commission to investigate how to make the states obey it, Madison eagerly joined. The delegates believed that Congress must have the power to tax, but many in the states wouldn't even consider giving it that right. Weren't they already fighting a war against a king who had taxed them too much?

Finally, a group of officers in the Continental Army brought on a crisis. Most of the fighting had ended in 1781, yet in January 1783, the officers still had not been paid for their years of service. They threatened to march on the Congress to demand payment. General George Washington persuaded the officers to remain patient, but faced with a rebellion, Congress was forced to act.

Madison and others introduced bills that would allow the Congress to raise money. Madison took a leading role in the debates. When the arguments grew bitter and positions hardened, Madison came up with a plan that allowed a compromise. After three years in Congress, he had learned to grasp complex issues and explain his position to others. He didn't use a booming voice or sweeping gestures to gain support. He didn't insult or talk down to his opponents. Instead, he carefully constructed his arguments. He was gracious, giving credit to his allies and sometimes flattering his enemies. If there were disagreements, he heard both sides and looked for a compromise.

When Madison, pale and small, began debating, he seemed to command little attention. He was the calm spot at the center of the political storm. But when the time came to vote, Madison's side almost always won.

Freeing a Slave

Madison had brought a slave named Billey to Philadelphia as a personal servant. When he returned to Virginia, he left Billey behind.

"I am persuaded his mind is too thoroughly tainted to be a fit companion for fellow slaves in Virginia," Madison wrote to his father. "I do not expect to get near the worth of him; but cannot think of punishing him by transportation merely for coveting that liberty for which we have paid the price of so much blood, and have proclaimed so often to be the right, and worthy the pursuit, of every human being."

Madison sold Billey to a Quaker. By Pennsylvania law, Quakers were required to free any slave after seven years. After that time, Billey was freed and took the last name of Gardner.

☆ ★ ☆

Chapter 2

A New National Challenge —————

Madison's experience and skill would be needed by the young nation. By 1783, the war was over and the British had recognized the independence of the United States. The Americans celebrated, but they also faced a new set of problems. Fighting and winning a war was one thing. The country's leaders now hoped to do something never done before—build a large nation where the people ruled themselves.

In Europe, many thought it couldn't be done. They said that a country's royalty and noble families knew best. They believed that common people—farmers, shoemakers, sailors, merchants, preachers—were not smart enough to participate in their own government. Such people couldn't be trusted to rule themselves. Europeans believed that forming a *republic*, in which a government relies on the agreement of common people, was a dream. A city or a small state might be able to form a republic, but no large nation had ever succeeded. The United States, they said, would surely fail.

In 1784, Madison might have agreed. He had left the Continental Congress and was serving in the Virginia state legislature. When the legislature debated giving more power to the national Congress, Madison couldn't persuade his fellow legislators to agree.

The problem was not just in Virginia. The states did not want to give up their own powers to a national government. With no war to fight, there was less reason than ever to work together. The states thought of themselves as separate countries. They issued their own money and controlled their own trade. Sometimes they charged *duties*, taxes on goods coming in from other states. They negotiated their own treaties with local Indian nations. No matter how Congress tried, the states would not work together. To Madison, it was clear that the Articles of Confederation were not working.

Between legislative sessions Madison returned to the family plantation at Montpelier, but plantation business didn't catch his imagination. He spent his time reading or riding horseback for hours, leaving others to manage the family's farms and businesses.

In the legislature, he became a leader once again. He took up a favorite cause—a bill that firmly established freedom of religion in Virginia. Madison defended his proposal even against the fiery orator Patrick Henry. Using his quiet powers of persuasion and reason, Madison finally prevailed and the bill passed.

Meanwhile, the Articles of Confederation were put to a harsh test. A farmer, Daniel Shays, led a rebellion against the state of Massachusetts. The national Congress wanted to help, but it still had no power to raise money or to call up an army for the common defense. Shays' Rebellion was short-lived, but the incident revealed again that the national government of the United States was weak.

The Constitution

Leaders throughout the states began calling for a meeting to reform the Articles. As a start, Madison and others called a meeting in 1786 in Annapolis, Maryland, to discuss trade among the states. Because delegates from only five states showed up, not much could be accomplished. Madison and Alexander Hamilton of New York called for another meeting. This one was scheduled to take place in Philadelphia and would discuss the Articles of Confederation.

The meeting, or convention, gained support through the states. In 1787, Madison was one of the 55 delegates who attended. Now 36 years old, Madison had enormous experience with government both as it was written about in books and as it worked in real life. He pored over texts that described how governments should work. He studied the problems state governments encountered during the Revolution. When Madison arrived in Philadelphia, he knew as much as any other delegate about the problems facing the government. He was also convinced he knew something else—how to solve them.

When independence was declared in 1776, the people of each state organized their own government. These first governments gave an enormous role to legislatures—or bodies of representatives elected directly by the people. Governors of the states weren't given much authority. Another part of the government—judges—wasn't given much attention either.

This was a mistake, Madison believed. The legislatures, it turned out, often acted hastily or not at all. When angry, they could make bad decisions without careful thought. At other times, they could argue bitterly about an important issue for years without taking action. Worst of all, a majority group in the legislature could pass laws that discriminated against a minority. The minority groups could lose their rights.

An artist's view of the Constitutional Convention. Washington, standing at the right, was the presiding officer. Madison, just to the left, kept a journal of the proceedings.

The states were discovering that they needed another powerful force to check the power of the legislature. A stronger governor could speak for all the people in the state, for minorities as well as for the majority. The governor could restrain the legislature when it moved too quickly or prod it when it moved too slowly.

Another problem was that legislatures sometimes passed laws that didn't make sense or conflicted with other laws already in place. After all, many members of the legislature were merchants and farmers, not lawyers. A stronger system of courts and judges could interpret the laws the legislature passed, pointing out cases where they did not make sense or conflicted with other laws.

Madison firmly believed that the United States needed a stronger federal government—one that could overrule state laws if necessary for the good of the whole nation. This would serve as another restraint on powerful state legislatures. He used the lessons from the early state governments in drawing up a plan for the new government. It provided for a government with three branches—the *legislature* (or congress), the *executive* (the president or governor), and the *judiciary* (the court system and its judges). The powers of each branch would balance the powers of the other branches. No one branch alone could make decisions that were vital to the country. When the three branches worked in harmony, Madison believed, the government would run smoothly and would not trample on the rights of states and individuals.

The Convention

On May 3, 1787, a coach carrying Madison and his books, clothes, and other goods pulled into Philadelphia. Eagerly, Madison prepared to begin work at the convention. But he soon discovered that starting work was impossible. Except for some Pennsylvania delegates, who didn't have far to travel, there was no one else there. Madison had arrived first. Madison took lodgings, read, wrote letters, and waited. He dined with Benjamin Franklin and viewed the beautiful Schuylkill River with George Washington. Gradually, delegates from other states began to arrive.

The delegates chose to meet in the Pennsylvania statehouse, a brick structure with a tall tower. The building—known today as Independence Hall—was already a part of history. More than ten years before, members of the Continental Congress had signed the Declaration of Independence within its walls.

Washington, the general of the American army throughout the Revolutionary War, was the convention's president. He sat at the front of the room in a large chair and recognized speakers during the debate. Madison, who was determined to take notes of the debates, sat directly in front of Washington. The 55 delegates who took their seats in the statehouse were among the most powerful and brilliant men in the states.

Even in this crowd, Madison stood out. "Every person seems to acknowledge his greatness," wrote William Pierce of Georgia. "The affairs of the United States, he perhaps has the most correct knowledge of, of any man in the Union."

The first order of business was to consider amending the Articles of Confederation. Many delegates believed that with some revisions it could continue to be the plan for the national government. After five days of debate, however, the convention agreed that the Articles were too flawed to be repaired. A completely new document would be needed.

Madison put forth his ideas for the new government in the "Virginia Plan." Many of the delegates were shocked at the breadth of his proposal. They agreed that changes were needed, but they questioned the need for such a powerful federal government.

The Virginia Plan was loudly opposed by the states with small populations. It provided that each state would have representatives to the new Congress in proportion to its population. Delegates from small states, such as New Jersey and Rhode Island, believed they would lose too much power to the larger states. Madison still insisted that representation be based on population, giving such states as Virginia, New York, and Pennsylvania most of the votes.

Madison was in the thick of the debates, speaking more than 120 times. He knew that sometimes he spoke too long. According to one story, he asked a friend to tug on his coat when he should sit down. Soon afterward, Madison got

Journal of the federal Convention Monday July 16. 1787.

The question being taken on the whole of the report from the grand Committee as amended

it passed in the affirmative and is as follows. namely.

Resolved — That in the original formation of the legislature of the United States the first Branch thereof shall consist of Sixty five members. of which number

New Hampshire shall send — Three
Massachusetts ——————— Eight
Rhode Island ——————— One
Connecticut ——————— Five
New York ——————— Six
New Jersey ——————— four
Pennsylvania ——————— Eight
Delaware ——————— One
Maryland ——————— Six
Virginia ——————— Ten
North Carolina ——————— Five
South Carolina ——————— Five
Georgia ——————— Three.

But as the present situation of the States may probably alter in the number of their inhabitants the legislature of the United States shall be authorised from time to time to apportion the number of representatives: and in case any of the States shall hereafter be divided, or enlarged by addition of territory; or any two or more States united, or any new States created within the limits of the United States the legislature of the United States shall possess authority to regulate the number of repre- -sentatives xxxx in xxxx any of the foregoing cases upon the principle of their number of inhabitants,

according

A page from Madison's journal of the debate. It includes a listing of states with the number of representatives they would have in the new House of Representatives, based on their populations.

excited and spoke until he was exhausted. He turned to his friend and asked him why he had not tugged on his coat.

"I would rather have laid a finger on the lightning," the friend answered.

The days dragged on, and so did the arguments. The pleasant spring weather turned into the heat of summer. The uncomfortable delegates debated day after day, keeping the windows closed so that passersby would not be able to listen. Afterward, they argued over candlelit card games in the coffeehouses and taverns of the city.

The small states wouldn't give in. Finally, the delegates hammered out a compromise. The legislature (or Congress) would be divided into two houses. In the House of Representatives, states would receive seats in proportion to their population. In the Senate, each state would have two seats, no matter how small or large its population was. This compromise was a serious defeat for Madison. Later, the convention rejected two more of his proposals to give the national government veto power over state laws. Deeply upset over setbacks, Madison began to wonder if the convention would succeed in forming a workable system.

There were still battles to be fought, however. Madison pushed his disappointment aside as the convention began to consider the executive branch—the office of the presidency. Madison argued for a strong executive, insisting that an independent leader elected by the people would balance the powers of the legislature. On this point Madison's views prevailed.

By early September, many delegates were impatient to get home. Fortunately, the new Constitution was nearly finished. On September 17, 1787, George Washington became the first to sign the finished document. Madison, like many others, was not entirely pleased with the document, but he signed it. Some of his cherished ideas had been rejected, but much of his plan had been adopted, including a government with three branches and a strong executive branch. He realized that the Constitution was a vast improvement over the Articles of Confederation.

Ratifying the Constitution

The new Constitution provided that it would become effective when special conventions in two-thirds of the states ratified it—nine of the thirteen. It was not certain that this would ever happen. Many citizens and states were distrustful of such a powerful central government. Though exhausted after five months of debates in the convention, Madison took a leading role in achieving the ratification of the Constitution.

The most famous defense of the Constitution appeared in a series of essays that appeared under the title *The Federalist*—as a supporter of

The last page of the finished Constitution, which includes the signatures of those participating in the convention. Madison's signature is in the left-hand column. He was one of two delegates from Virginia to sign it.

the Constitution was known. The 85 *Federalist* essays were not signed, but historians believe that Madison wrote between 25 and 30 of them. John Jay of New York wrote 5, and all the rest—between 50 and 55—were written by Alexander Hamilton. Madison's essays address the critics of the Constitution and review their arguments, persuading readers that the Constitution's plan is sound and will work. *The Federalist* is still read and admired today by students of political philosophy and by judges wanting to know what the framers of the Constitution intended.

Madison didn't confine his campaign to writing essays. Perhaps his biggest battle was in Virginia, where many in the special convention to consider the Constitution planned to vote against it. Madison worked tirelessly to persuade the delegates to approve the

THE

FEDERALIST:

A COLLECTION

O F

E S S A Y S,

WRITTEN IN FAVOUR OF THE

NEW CONSTITUTION,

AS AGREED UPON BY THE FEDERAL CONVENTION,
SEPTEMBER 17, 1787.

IN TWO VOLUMES.

V O L. I.

N E W - Y O R K:

PRINTED AND SOLD BY J. AND A. M'LEAN,
No. 41, HANOVER-SQUARE,
M,DCC,LXXXVIII.

The title page of the collected *Federalist* essays "written in favour of the new Constitution." The essays were written by Alexander Hamilton, Madison, and John Jay.

document. His old opponent Patrick Henry spoke eloquently in favor of a less powerful federal government. Another opponent was a young Virginian named James Monroe, who would later become one of Madison's closest political allies. When the Constitution was put to the vote, once again Madison's side was victorious. Virginia was the tenth state to ratify the Constitution, on June 25, 1788.

Madison and the other members of the Constitutional Convention made one important concession that helped assure ratification. Critics of the Constitution complained that it did not have a *bill of rights*—a clear listing of essential rights of individuals and states. The framers agreed that this criticism was fair and promised that a bill of rights would be added to the Constitution in the early days of the new government. One state, North Carolina, ratified the Constitution conditionally—only if a bill of rights was added.

Madison was not much concerned about a bill of rights at first, believing that state guarantees were enough. Then, in the first congressional elections, he ran against James Monroe, his opponent from the Virginia ratifying convention. He realized that a bill of rights was important to voters, representing a clear statement by the new federal government that basic human rights would be respected.

Madison himself drafted the Bill of Rights, drawing from an earlier version written by George Mason for the Virginia constitution in 1776. These guarantees were enacted as the first ten amendments to the Constitution. They were ratified by the states and took effect in December 1791.

The long task of planning a new government was finished. Now it was time to see if the government would work. Madison, one of the most experienced and respected members of the Congress, turned his attention to helping run the new nation.

Chapter 3

Working Behind the Scenes ———————

When the first government under the Constitution gathered in 1789 in New York City—the nation's temporary capital—Madison was an insider. He was a member of Congress. George Washington, the new president, asked advice and relied on his writing skills. His close friend Thomas Jefferson was the secretary of state. Alexander Hamilton, with whom Madison had written *The Federalist*, was secretary of the treasury.

Madison continued to perform most of his best work privately, outside the spotlight. He drafted Washington's first inaugural address to Congress. As a member and a leader of the House of Representatives, Madison wrote the congressional response to Washington's address. Then he drafted Washington's thank-you letter to Congress!

One of the first issues the new government had to face was a huge debt. The federal government and the states had not repaid loans from foreign governments made during the Revolutionary War, which had ended nearly six years earlier. The governments also owed money to men who had served in the Continental Army and in the state militias. Secretary of the Treasury Alexander Hamilton estimated that the total debt was $77.1 million, a huge sum at the time. In January 1790, he presented a plan to reorganize the country's finances. He proposed that the national government take responsibility for its own debts and all state debts from the war. To pay the debts, the treasury could raise money from individuals and businesses by selling bonds. In effect, the government would borrow money from the bondholders, offering to repay them with interest. The money raised could also be used for new projects that would benefit the whole nation.

Madison and many others opposed Hamilton's plan. Some of the states, including Virginia, had already paid off their debts. Why should the national government have to go into debt because some states still owed money? Madison also believed the plan would be unfair to many Revolutionary soldiers. They had been "paid" with certificates that promised later payment of a certain amount. Because the soldiers couldn't wait years for the money, they had sold these certificates to speculators for a fraction of the amount the certificates promised. If the government now paid the full amount, the soldiers would get nothing more, but the speculators would get rich.

A second important issue for the government was the location of the national capital. The government met first in New York and later in Philadelphia. The northern states favored keeping it in one of these northern cities. Madison, Jefferson, and many others from southern states wanted a capital nearer the south.

In 1790, Hamilton and Jefferson came to a compromise that addressed both issues. Jefferson and his followers agreed to support Hamilton's economic plan, while Hamilton and his followers agreed to establish a new capital city on the Potomac River, on the border between Maryland and Virginia. After much debate, the compromise was passed by both houses of Congress.

Madison was pleased that these problems had been solved. Yet he and Jefferson found themselves more and more opposed to Hamilton's further plans, which called for the central government to exercise still greater economic power. In Congress, Madison led the debate against Hamilton's proposals.

When Madison and Hamilton had worked together in urging states to ratify the Constitution, Madison agreed with Hamilton in favoring a strong central government. Now it seemed to him that Hamilton's proposals went beyond the powers given the federal government in the Constitution. The Hamilton plan seemed to favor wealthy merchants and traders, most of whom lived in the north,

Thomas Jefferson (above) and Alexander Hamilton (right) were both in Washington's cabinet. Their disagreements led to the creation of the first political parties. Madison sided with Jefferson and helped establish the Democratic-Republican party.

and to work against small farmers and businessmen in the south and west. Madison came to agree with Jefferson, who mistrusted the central government and believed that many powers should be left to state and local governments. Together, Jefferson and Madison began to organize a "faction," which gradually developed into a political party. Its members became known as Democratic-Republicans; Hamilton's supporters were known as Federalists for their support of greater power for the federal government.

International Strife

As the new government debated, Europe was in the midst of revolution and war. In 1789, the first year of Washington's presidency, French citizens rose against the oppressive government of their monarch, King Louis XVI. At first, many in the United States rejoiced. The French Revolution seemed to carry on the work of the American Revolution, ending a system in which a royal family and a small number of noble families controlled a country's politics, owned most of its land, and often oppressed the common people.

Soon, however, the French Revolution brought *anarchy*—complete disorder and lawlessness—instead of reform. Moderate reformers were thrown out of office and executed, and new leaders ruled more by terror than by law. King Louis and his queen, Marie Antoinette, were taken prisoner and executed. Britain

Citizens of Paris storm the Bastille, a castle that served as a prison, on July 14, 1789, beginning the French Revolution.

saw the new French government as a dangerous enemy, and in 1793 the countries went to war. People and leaders in the United States debated the meaning of this increasingly violent revolution, some arguing in favor of the French Republic and others in favor of Britain.

The United States was caught in the middle. Its merchant ships carried goods to both sides. Both Britain and France demanded that trade with their enemy be halted. Then both began to seize American merchant ships. The powerful British navy boarded American vessels even in the West Indies and *impressed* American sailors—forced them to become crewmen on British warships. Americans were enraged, and it appeared that the two nations might soon be at war once again.

Impressment: Who Was Right?

When the British navy stopped American ships, they would impress some of the sailors—force them to become crewmen on navy ships. The British officers claimed that the sailors had deserted the British navy. Americans complained loudly that their rights were being violated. Yet many British sailors had left harsh conditions in the British navy to serve on American merchant ships. Britain also justified impressment by the theory of "perpetual allegiance." They said that any sailor born in Britain continued to owe allegiance to the country, even though he may have lived in the United States from boyhood or become an American citizen.

☆ ☆ ☆

Marriage

Despite these developments, Madison found time to devote to his personal life. In 1793, he met a young widow, Dolley Payne Todd. During that year, Dolley's husband and her younger son had died in a yellow fever epidemic. She was left with one son, John Payne Todd, who was still a toddler. Mrs. Todd had been raised in Virginia in a Quaker family, which moved to Philadelphia ten years earlier when she was a teenager.

At 25, Dolley Todd was 17 years younger than Madison, but he was attracted to her outgoing personality, her lively wit, and her intelligence. The next

Dolley Madison, the charming young woman James Madison married in 1794.

year, Madison made a proposal of marriage. The couple was married on September 15, 1794, at the Virginia estate of Dolley's younger sister. By October, the couple had returned to Philadelphia.

Jay's Treaty

President Washington's cabinet was increasingly split between the Federalists, who favored closer relations with Britain, and the Democratic-Republicans, who continued to support France and its revolution. In 1794, Washington sent James Monroe, a Democratic-Republican, to France to improve relations with that country and sent Federalist John Jay to Britain. In November, John Jay signed a treaty with England to preserve peace. When it was presented to the Senate for ratification in 1795, the treaty caused an uproar. It appeared to give Britain a huge advantage over France, and worst of all, it did not require Britain to stop attacking American merchant ships and impressing sailors. To Jay and George Washington, the treaty was necessary to keep peace. They believed that the young United States was not ready or able to fight a second war with Britain. The treaty was ratified by the Senate in June 1795. Yet the bruising conflict over the issue was so great that both Hamilton and Jefferson resigned from the cabinet.

Madison introduced a bill in the House of Representatives challenging the treaty, hoping that the government would withdraw it. After further heated debate, the Federalists voted down Madison's bill in April 1796. Later that year, George Washington retired, and his vice president, Federalist John Adams, was elected president over the Democratic-Republican candidate, Thomas Jefferson.

Madison was extremely discouraged. During nearly eight years in Congress, he had been unable to defeat the Federalists. In the spring of 1797, he retired from Congress and returned with Dolley to Montpelier.

Montpelier and Controversy ——————

Madison's estate at Montpelier was a thriving farm with a handsome mansion and views of the Blue Ridge Mountains in the distance. Madison had spent much of his adult life in the halls of government, but now he threw himself into his new life as a gentleman farmer. He read journals and books on the latest agricultural practices and exchanged letters with Jefferson and others discussing farm improvements. He also heard from his political friends in Philadelphia, where President Adams was running into trouble.

Jay's Treaty had angered the government of France, which had believed that the United States would be an ally, not an enemy. France began seizing American ships. Later, it insulted American diplomats who had been sent to improve relations. The French minister for foreign affairs refused to see them for months. Then French politicians suggested that talks might be arranged after payment of a huge bribe. Public opinion in the United States suddenly swung against France, and some talked of war. Adams suggested to Jefferson that Madison be sent to France to ease the dangerous situation. Madison refused the appointment, pleading that he was too frail to survive such a long journey.

With war with France now threatening, Federalists in Congress proposed harsh new laws restricting *aliens* (foreign-born immigrants and visitors) and punishing *sedition* (speaking against the government). Adams signed these Alien and Sedition Acts into law.

Madison and Jefferson were horrified by the sedition acts, which made it a criminal offense to question government actions. The acts seemed to deny citizens freedom of speech, which was a right promised by the First Amendment of the Constitution. Madison drafted a resolution for the Virginia legislature opposing the Alien and Sedition Acts and defending the right of free speech. Yet when some legislators called for the states to disobey the national laws, Madison disagreed. The laws of the land must be obeyed by all, he said, even if one or another seems unjust. The solution, he thought, was to win the presidency from the Federalists.

Secretary of State

The election of 1800 was a bitter confrontation between the Federalists and the growing Democratic-Republican party. Federalist John Adams was running for reelection. The Democratic-Republican candidate was Thomas Jefferson, and James Madison was a leading force in his campaign.

When the electoral college met to cast its votes, there was no doubt that Madison's and Jefferson's party had won. However, Jefferson was tied in electoral votes with his own vice-presidential candidate, Aaron Burr. The election was settled in the House of Representatives, which finally elected Jefferson.

Jefferson asked Madison to be his secretary of state. After four years at Montpelier, Madison was ready to return to politics. He and Dolley packed up and were soon traveling to the nation's new capital city—Washington, D.C.

Though the plans for the great city had already been drawn, little had actually been done on the site. When the Madisons arrived, there were wide avenues, but few buildings. Most of it was a patchwork of fields and swamp, rolling hills and forests. Madison and Dolley moved into a newly built three-story brick house, just down the street from the Executive Mansion, where the president lived. Madison was often at the mansion.

Jefferson was eight years older than Madison, but they had similar backgrounds and shared devotion both to the new United States and to their home state of Virginia. They had worked together for years and had become close friends. During Jefferson's eight years as president, Madison was his closest adviser.

When James and Dolley Madison moved to Washington in 1801, it was still a small city. Major government buildings were only being planned or were under construction.

Together, they worked to preserve peace with both France and England. France was now ruled by Napoleon Bonaparte, who had taken dictatorial powers and began threatening to wage war on neighboring countries. Jefferson and Madison learned that Spain had given its Louisiana Territory in North America to France, raising fear that Napoleon might close the Mississippi River to American shipping or even seek a war in North America. They sent James Monroe to Paris in 1803 with an offer from the United States to buy New Orleans. Napoleon, who needed money for his military campaigns in Europe, surprised the Americans by offering the whole Louisiana Territory, an area that would double the size of the United States. Monroe agreed. Jefferson and Madison gained the approval of Congress.

Then a new war broke out between France and England. Again, the United States was caught in the middle. British and French warships stopped American merchant ships, seizing goods and impressing sailors. Britain's great navy ruled the ocean, and Americans would have to carry on trade according to British rules.

On June 22, 1807, the American frigate *Chesapeake* was stopped by a British warship, the *Leopard*, off the coast of Virginia. The *Leopard* fired its cannons, raking the ship with shot. The British then boarded the *Chesapeake* and

British sailors from the *Leopard* board the U.S. ship *Chesapeake* after firing on her in 1807 off the coast of Virginia. The incident nearly caused war between the two countries.

took three American sailors that they claimed were deserters. News of the attack, so near the U.S. coast, caused rage through the states.

In retaliation for the *Chesapeake* affair, Jefferson and Madison encouraged Congress to pass an *embargo*, providing that no American ships could carry American goods to England or France. The act passed late in 1807, and

Jefferson signed it into law. He hoped that the loss of U.S. goods would be painful to the European powers and would force them to respect the rights of the United States.

By summer 1808, it was clear that the embargo was a failure. Britain and France found needed goods from other countries, while hundreds of American ships sat in port. Merchants went bankrupt, and sailors' families faced starvation.

Jefferson and Madison declared an embargo, making it illegal to ship goods to Britain or France. The embargo caused a serious recession. In this cartoon, Jefferson defends his policy against a crowd of protesters.

Farmers who sold grain to Europe saw prices drop sharply. An outcry arose in the country. Jefferson signed a bill ending the embargo early in 1809, four days before leaving office.

President Madison

Following the example of George Washington, Jefferson announced in 1808 that he would not run for a third term. Madison, his closest adviser, was nominated by the Democratic-Republican party. He was easily elected, defeating the Federalist candidate Charles Pinckney.

On March 4, 1809, Madison, nearly 58 years old, took the oath of office, becoming the fourth president of the United States. He rode to the Capitol building in a horse and carriage accompanied by a unit of cavalry and took the oath in a crowded House of Representatives. Jefferson, who was observing, felt "like a prisoner released from his chains."

Madison and Dolley returned to the Executive Mansion, where they received well-wishers. Margaret Bayard Smith described the reception in a letter: "The street was full of carriages and people, and we had to wait for near half an hour before we could get in. The house was completely filled, parlours, entry, drawing room, and bed room. Near to the door of the drawing room, Mr. and Mrs. Madison stood to receive their company. She looked extremely beautiful, was dressed in a plain dress with a very long train, plain round the neck without any handkerchief, and beautiful bonnet of purple velvet, and white satin with white plumes. She was all dignity, grace and affability. . . . The crowd was immense both at the Capitol and here, thousands and thousands of people thronged the avenue."

The presidency of James Madison had begun.

Chapter 4

Trouble at Home and Abroad

As president, Madison found himself in an unfamiliar situation. For many years he had worked behind the scenes to accomplish things as a congressional leader and as Jefferson's secretary of state. Now, as president, he was expected to take the lead publicly. He found that many in Congress did not want to be led by a president at all. His biggest problem was with his own party. The Federalists had few votes in Congress and lacked a strong leader. Their founder, Alexander Hamilton, had been killed in a duel in 1804. With no strong opposition party, the Democratic-Republicans had begun to fight among themselves.

The big issue facing the government was the same one that had occupied Jefferson—dealing with the attacks of British and French warships on American merchant ships. Britain and France

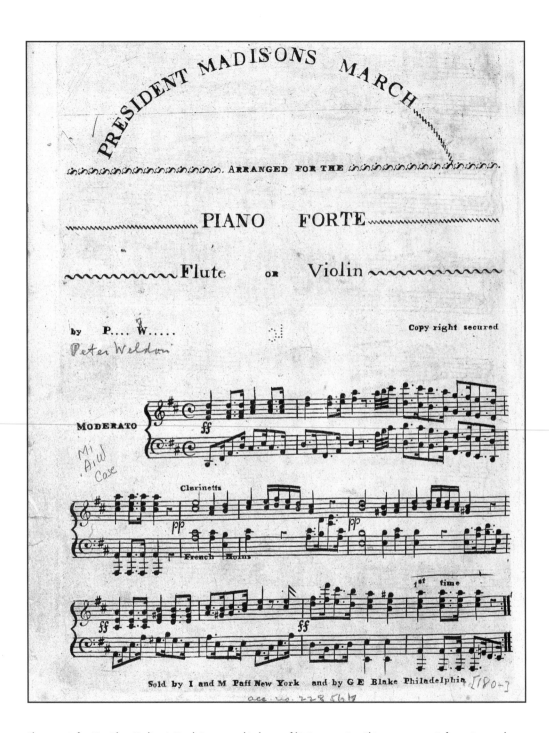

Sheet music for "President Madison's March," composed in honor of his inauguration. This arrangement is for a piano and a flute or violin.

both imposed blockades against the other, making it more and more difficult for American merchant ships to carry their goods to Europe and sell them. The British continued to board American ships and to take sailors they claimed were deserters from the British navy. Meanwhile, in the west, the British claimed lands south of the Great Lakes and were arming and supporting Indian tribes who were fighting American settlers. In Congress, many wanted to declare war on Britain, but others—especially the merchants in New England—wanted to make peace with Britain so that trade could resume.

Tippecanoe

As more and more American settlers arrived in the Indiana Territory after 1800, dealings with the Native Americans there became strained. Some groups agreed to sign treaties and move to the west, but others refused. The strongest resister was Tecumseh, a Shawnee chief who hoped to unify tribes in the region to resist the American settlers. He received support from the British in Canada. In 1811, the governor of the Indiana Territory, William Henry Harrison, marched American troops to Tecumseh's stronghold on the Tippecanoe River. The Shawnee attacked, killing many Americans, but were forced to retreat when they ran out of ammunition. Harrison occupied the Indian settlement and claimed victory. Years later, Harrison would win the presidency largely because of the reputation he made at Tippecanoe.

☆ ☆ ☆

In the congressional elections of 1810, many Republican "War Hawks" were elected. Mostly from western and southern states, they pressed Madison to declare war on Britain. They talked of invading British Canada and West Florida, the territory along the Gulf of Mexico claimed by Spain, then Britain's ally. Madison asked Congress to build up the army and especially the navy. The War Hawks wanted war, but they were reluctant to increase taxes to build new ships. The British and French, locked in battle in Europe, paid little attention to the growing pressure for war in the United States.

Finally, on June 1, 1812, Madison asked Congress for a declaration of war against Britain. The war resolution passed, but fewer than 100 congressmen voted in favor while 62 voted against. Madison formally declared war on June 18.

War

The conflict known as the War of 1812 started badly for the United States. The country was poorly prepared. Experienced military leaders were scarce, and the standing army was small. The state militias, groups of farmers and merchants who drilled on weekends, were poorly trained. Because Congress was reluctant to spend money, the army had few weapons, little gunpowder, and almost no equipment.

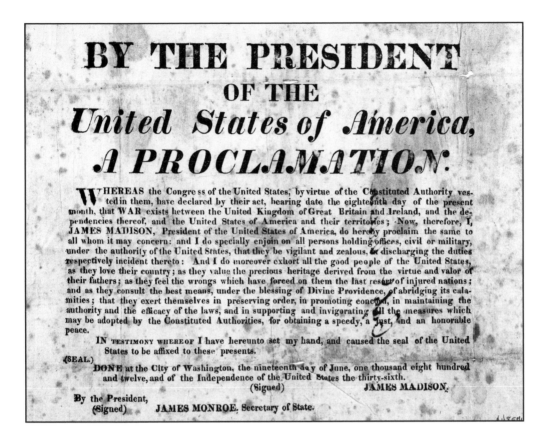

BY THE PRESIDENT
OF THE
United States of America,
A PROCLAMATION.

WHEREAS the Congress of the United States, by virtue of the Constituted Authority vested in them, have declared by their act, bearing date the eighteenth day of the present month, that WAR exists between the United Kingdom of Great Britain and Ireland, and the dependencies thereof, and the United States of America and their territories; Now, therefore, I, JAMES MADISON, President of the United States of America, do hereby proclaim the same to all whom it may concern: and I do specially enjoin on all persons holding offices, civil or military, under the authority of the United States, that they be vigilant and zealous, in discharging the duties respectively incident thereto: And I do moreover exhort all the good people of the United States, as they love their country; as they value the precious heritage derived from the virtue and valor of their fathers; as they feel the wrongs which have forced on them the last resort of injured nations; and as they consult the best means, under the blessing of Divine Providence, of abridging its calamities; that they exert themselves in preserving order, in promoting concord, in maintaining the authority and the efficacy of the laws, and in supporting and invigorating all the measures which may be adopted by the Constituted Authorities, for obtaining a speedy, a just, and an honorable peace.

IN TESTIMONY WHEREOF I have hereunto set my hand, and caused the seal of the United States to be affixed to these presents.

(SEAL.)

DONE at the City of Washington, the nineteenth day of June, one thousand eight hundred and twelve, and of the Independence of the United States the thirty-sixth.

(Signed)   JAMES MADISON.

By the President,
(Signed)   JAMES MONROE, Secretary of State.

In June 1812, after Congress declared war on Great Britain, Madison issued this proclamation, which was widely published.

Worse, not everyone agreed that the country should have started the war at all. In New England, many feared that war would cause even further damage to their economy. The governors of Massachusetts, Rhode Island, and Connecticut refused to let their militias join a crucial campaign against Canada.

Madison hoped for a quick victory. American forces could quickly march into Canada and capture British forts. Once the British had lost control of their

What: Also known as the Second War of Independence

When: 1812–1814

Who: The United States against Great Britain

Where: In the United States, Canada, and on the Atlantic Ocean

Why: Americans were angry that Britain was restricting U.S. shipping, seizing cargoes and sailors from U.S. ships, and encouraging Northwest Indians to attack American settlements.

Outcome: On the ground and at sea, the war was inconclusive. In the 1814 Treaty of Ghent (signed in December 1814), both sides agreed to end the war. Britain agreed to end impressment of American seamen and give up British forts in the Northwest Territory of the U.S. The treaty also settled disputes about U.S. fishing rights in Canadian waters, about naval forces on the Great Lakes, and about commercial relations between the two countries.

North American bases, thought Madison, they would be forced to negotiate. His hopes were soon dashed. In August 1812, the British and their Indian allies captured Fort Dearborn (now Chicago), then forced American general William Hull to surrender his 2,000-man army to a smaller British force at Detroit. In October, an American force invaded Canada, crossing the Niagara River, but was defeated at Queenston. Soon afterward, another U.S. invading force stopped at the border when militiamen refused to march into Canada.

The Naval War

The Americans' only source of encouragement came from the naval war. The British navy was the most powerful in the world. It counted 191 ships of the line, giant craft that carried 60 to 90 guns each. It also had 245 smaller frigates, which were still formidable with 30 to 50 guns each. The American navy, by contrast, began the war with only seven frigates, but these ships were expertly designed and manned. They carried more men and guns than normal frigates. They were also faster, steered easily, and were protected by heavy oak siding.

Manned by excellent sailors and bold captains, they became a deadly nuisance to the British fleet. On August 19, 1812, the *U.S.S. Constitution* spotted the British frigate *Guerriere*. The two ships pounded each other with cannon fire. The

The U.S frigate *Constitution* (right) met the British warship *Guerriere* off the coast of Newfoundland in August 1812 and destroyed it in one of the few early victories for the United States in the War of 1812.

The States During the Presidency of James Madison

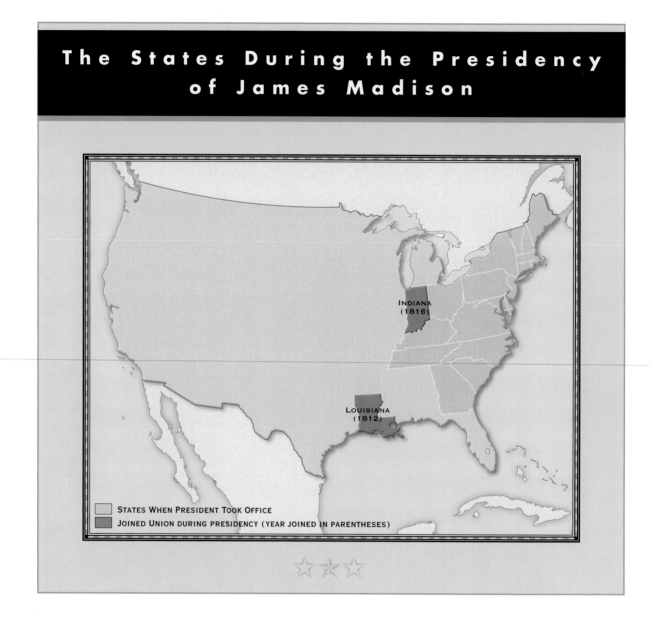

INDIANA
(1816)

LOUISIANA
(1812)

STATES WHEN PRESIDENT TOOK OFFICE
JOINED UNION DURING PRESIDENCY (YEAR JOINED IN PARENTHESES)

British were shocked to see their cannonballs bounce harmlessly off the *Constitution*'s hull. Within hours, the *Guerriere*'s masts had fallen into the sea, and the ship lay helpless.

American ships would have a series of such victories, stunning the British and cheering the Americans. Considering the size of the British navy, the American victories were not very important, but they provided some good news for worried citizens at home and showed that the United States could turn the tables on the British.

Reelection

In the midst of war, Madison faced reelection. The Federalists nominated DeWitt Clinton of New York, but their party was deeply divided, especially on the issue of the war. Madison was reelected easily. His real opposition continued to come from within his own party.

Meanwhile, the Executive Mansion became a glittering social attraction in Washington, thanks largely to Dolley Madison. She planned dinners and receptions where she and the president could entertain foreign visitors and diplomats, leaders of government departments, and members of Congress. Dolley was warm and witty and was soon greatly admired in the city. She was a striking contrast to her husband, who was quiet and withdrawn and usually dressed in black. An English visitor described him as a schoolteacher dressed up for a funeral. Dolley's receptions and dinners were more than just times for recreation and pleasure. They gave James a chance to meet many influential people and talk over important issues.

Chapter 5

Second Term

A Seesaw War

In 1813, the Americans heard some encouraging news of the war. Navy commander Oliver Hazard Perry and his men built a fleet of small warships on the shore of Lake Erie, defeated a British force and took control of the lake. In a message to army commanders on land, Perry wrote, "We have met the enemy and he is ours." His victory made it possible for William Henry Harrison (of Tippecanoe fame) to recapture Detroit and score a major victory over a British army at Thames River in present-day Ontario.

Americans also sowed the seeds of later disasters. Late in 1813, they captured York (present-day Toronto) and burned the Parliament building of Upper Canada. This needless destruction infuriated the British. Soon afterward, they captured and burned settle-

"Don't Give Up the Ship!"

Oliver Hazard Perry flew a special flag as he sailed into battle with the British on Lake Erie in September 1813. Earlier that year, Perry's friend James Lawrence, captain of the *U.S.S. Chesapeake*, was wounded during a naval battle in the Atlantic. Near death, Lawrence gave his crew one last command—"Don't give up the ship!" Perry had Lawrence's words stitched in white letters on a large blue flag. Ever since, the words have served as an inspiration in the U.S. navy.

★★☆

ments on the American side of the Niagara River, including the village of Buffalo. The next year they would get an even greater revenge.

By 1814, British ships cruised up and down the coast off the United States, blocking all trade and attacking cities. American warships continued to win some stirring victories in close combat, but the U.S. navy was no match for the large and powerful British navy.

In 1813, a fleet commanded by Oliver Hazard Perry defeated a British fleet in the Battle of Lake Erie. This proved to be a major victory for the United States, allowing it to recapture Detroit and pursue a British army into Canada.

Madison, frustrated by Congress, could hardly keep his own cabinet together. When he ordered his secretary of war to prepare to defend Washington, the secretary ignored the request. In New England, resistance to the war grew greater with each passing month. Shipping and trade were the economic life of the region, and the war meant that even more ships sat useless in harbors and that goods made for sale in Europe sat unsold. New England critics railed against what they called "Mr. Madison's War." Some even considered seceding from the Union.

In August, a large British army landed just 35 miles from Washington. It marched overland, scattering poorly prepared American militia units. Madison personally watched the British forces easily push aside the last American defenses. He then fled into Virginia. Dolley Madison remained at the mansion, using a telescope to watch the events. As the British came closer, she loaded her carriage full of personal belongings. At the last minute, she took a famous Gilbert Stuart painting of George Washington out of its frame and gave it to friends to hide safely. Then her carriage pulled away.

Behind her, the British troops were rampaging through Washington. British admiral George Cockburn told fleeing citizens, "You may thank old Madison for this. It is he who got you into this scrape."

Cockburn entered the Executive Mansion. He poured a glass of the president's wine and offered a mocking toast to Madison—"Jemmy's health!" Then

British admiral Cockburn, who led troops into Washington, captured the deserted Executive Mansion. In Madison's office, he stood on Madison's chair and proposed a sarcastic toast to "Jemmy's [James Madison's] health!"

his troops set fire to the mansion and many other government buildings in the city, including the Capitol and the Library of Congress. By morning, they were charred, smoldering shells.

For the destruction of Washington, Madison might have found himself in deep trouble as president. Three weeks later, however, when the British tried to capture Baltimore, they were defeated and forced to withdraw. At about the same

The Star-Spangled Banner

Francis Scott Key watched the British bombardment of Fort McHenry in the Baltimore harbor from a ship. He knew that if the U.S. flag still flew over the fort, the Americans were still unbeaten. The verses he wrote about the battle later became the national anthem of the United States. The familiar first verse describes the scene:

O say, can you see by the dawn's early light

What so proudly we hailed at the twilight's last gleaming,

Whose broad stripes and bright stars through the perilous fight

O'er the ramparts we watched were so gallantly streaming?

And the rockets' red glare, the bombs bursting in air,

Gave proof through the night that our flag was still there.

Oh say, does that Star-Spangled Banner yet wave

O'er the land of the free and the home of the brave?

☆☆☆

time in northern New York, American forces turned back a British army marching south from Canada.

Victory and Peace ———————————————

Negotiations to end the war had already begun in August 1814 in Ghent (in present-day Belgium). At first the British demanded concessions from the Americans, feeling that they had won the war. When news of the defeats in Baltimore and northern New York arrived, however, they dropped their demands. The negotiator for the United States was John Quincy Adams, son of President John Adams and a future president himself.

Even as Madison awaited news of the negotiations, the war continued. A large British army was in the Gulf of Mexico, sailing toward New Orleans, at the mouth of the Mississippi River. If the British captured this port city, the produce of farmers in the western states would be cut off from shipment and trade. An American force, led by Andrew Jackson, prepared to defend the city. Jackson's men built earthen walls at a narrow point between the Mississippi and a swamp. On January 8, 1815, the British attacked. When Jackson gave the order, cannon shells began punching holes in the British lines. Then the American soldiers stood and raked them with musket fire. British soldiers fell by the hundreds, but they pressed their attacks. By the end of the day, 192 had died, more than 1,265 were

Andrew Jackson (on horse at far right) watches as his troops drive the British back at the Battle of New Orleans.

wounded, and nearly 500 missing, yet they had not broken the American defenses. The Americans suffered only 13 dead, 13 wounded, and 19 missing. The British retreated to their ships.

Just as the news of the shattering victory at New Orleans arrived in Washington, a New England delegation arrived in the city to discuss its anger with the war. As a Frenchman observed, "Their position was awkward, embarrassing, and lent itself to cruel ridicule."

Madison was delighted to receive more news, this time from Ghent. He learned that a treaty had been signed on December 24, 1814, two weeks before the Battle of New Orleans. Both sides had agreed to return territory that their armies then occupied and to keep boundaries where they had been before the war. The treaty was ratified by the U.S. Senate in February. The War of 1812 was over.

The Fruits of Peace ─────────────────

After six years in the presidency, nearly three years of it at war, Madison could at last relax. He had been severely criticized by his enemies and allies; the war had been poorly led and poorly run. Yet when it was over, Americans everywhere took heart. They had fought England, the most powerful nation on earth, and had not lost. The American navy had won several victories. At New Orleans a brave American army had heroically defeated a British army. Madison, who had been

Evening Gazette Office,

Boston, Monday, 10, a.m.

The following most highly important handbill has just been issued from the Centinel press. We deem a duty that we owe our Friends and the Public to assist in the prompt spread of the Glorious News.

Treaty of PEACE signed and arrived.

Centinel Office, Feb. 13, 1815, 8 o'clock in the morning.

WE have this instant received in Thirty-two hours from New-York the following

Great and Happy News!

FOR THE PUBLIC.

To BENJAMIN RUSSELL, Esq. Centinel Office, Boston.

New-York, Feb. 11, 1815—Saturday Evening, 10 o'clock.

SIR—

I HASTEN to acquaint you, for the information of the Public, of the arrival here this afternoon of H. Br. M. sloop of war *Favorite*, in which has come passenger Mr. CARROLL, American Messenger, having in his possession

A Treaty of Peace

Between this Country and Great-Britain, signed on the 26th December last.

Mr. Baker also is on board, as Agent for the British Government, the same who was formerly Charge des Affairs here.

Mr. Carroll reached town at eight o'clock this evening. He shewed to a friend of mine, who is acquainted with him, the packet containing the *Treaty*, and a London newspaper of the last date of December, announcing the signing of the Treaty.

It depends, however, as my friend observed, upon the act of the President to suspend hostilities on this side.

The gentleman left London the 2d Jan. The *Transit* had sailed previously from a port on the Continent.

This city is in a perfect uproar of joy, shouts, illuminations, &c. &c.

I have undertaken to send you this by Express—the rider engaging to deliver it by Eight o'clock on Monday morning. The expense will be 225 dollars.—If you can collect so much to indemnify me I will thank you to do so.

I am with respect, Sir, your obedient servant,

JONATHAN GOODHUE.

We most heartily felicitate our Country on this auspicious news, which may be relied on as wholly authentic—Centinel.

PEACE EXTRA.

A handbill announces to the people of Boston that the War of 1812 is over. The Treaty of Ghent was signed in December, but the news did not reach Boston until February 13!

blamed for the war when it went badly, now received the credit when it ended on a positive note. For the first time he became a popular president.

Madison could finally direct his attention to issues within the nation. Instead of worrying about guns and supplies for soldiers, he proposed the building of roads and canals and the establishment of a national university (which had also been a dream of George Washington's).

Still, the stresses of the war had changed Madison and his party. They had stood for a government with limited powers, yet the wartime federal government gained power at the expense of the states. The Democratic-Republicans' ideal state was a nation of small farmers who would participate in local government and help govern themselves, yet the war had led to the development of more factories and the growth of cities.

Like Washington and Jefferson, Madison was content to serve for two terms. In 1816, the Democratic-Republicans nominated Madison's secretary of state James Monroe for president. The Federalists, discredited because of their heated opposition to the war, ran only a halfhearted campaign. In the electoral college Monroe received 184 votes to the Federalists' 34. On March 4, 1817, Madison watched with satisfaction as James Monroe was sworn in as fifth president of the United States.

On April 6, Madison and his wife boarded a steamboat and left Washington, D.C. Madison was happy to leave behind the strains of being president. An observer recalled that he was "as playful as a child who talked and joked with everyone on board, and reminded me of a schoolboy on a long vacation."

Chapter 6

Home at Last

Since 1801, Madison had never spent more than a few months each year at Montpelier. By summer 1817, he made it home once again. He turned again to reading books, writing letters, and running the farm. His friend Thomas Jefferson once called him the best farmer in Virginia. Still, Madison faced the problems of a plantation economy. Although he was rich in land and it produced fine crops, he could not always sell them at a profit, and sometimes cash was scarce.

Over the years, Madison watched with pride as the nation grew. The Constitution, which he had done so much to create, continued to be the law of the land. Settlers pushed farther to the west, and new roads and canals helped increase travel and trade. Yet there were signs of trouble as conflict grew between northern and southern states.

James Madison in a copy of a portrait by Gilbert Stuart.

Wrestling with Slavery

One of the main causes of the conflict was the institution of slavery. Like George Washington and Thomas Jefferson, Madison owned slaves. About a hundred lived and worked at Montpelier. They counted as part of his wealth, allowing him to cultivate a large plantation in a day before laborsaving machines. Slavery was a fact of life—and an important part of a plantation's economy. However, he was uncomfortable with slavery. If "all men are created equal," as Jefferson had written in the Declaration of Independence, what about the black men and women who washed his clothes, cooked his food, and worked in his fields? He once wrote that slavery was base and evil, and he searched for a solution to the problem. Like many others of his time, he thought slaves might be transported back to Africa, where they could establish communities of their own. What seemed impossible to him and to other southerners at the time was that slaves could live as free men and women in the United States.

Tragically, neither Madison nor any of the country's early leaders could find a solution to the problem of slavery. After his presidency, the nation would wrestle with it for nearly fifty years, finding the answer only through the destruction and bloodshed of the Civil War.

The Last Survivor

The years passed. Thomas Jefferson and John Adams both died on July 4, 1826. By the time Madison turned 80 in 1831, he was shocked to realize that he was the last of the Revolutionary leaders still alive.

"Having outlived so many of my contemporaries," he wrote, "I ought not to forget that I may be thought to have outlived myself."

Madison lived for another five years, spending all of his time at Montpelier. As she had in Washington, Dolley held parties and entertained guests. When Madison could no longer write because of arthritis, Dolley wrote for him.

On June 28, 1836, Madison's niece was sitting with him at breakfast. She noticed his expression suddenly alter and asked if something was wrong.

"Nothing more than a change of mind, my dear," he replied. Seconds later, he was dead. He was 85. Madison was buried in the family plot on the plantation. Dolley later sold Montpelier and moved back to Washington, D.C. She died there in 1849 at the age of 81.

Madison's Legacy

Any American student can name George Washington, Thomas Jefferson, and Benjamin Franklin as Founding Fathers—brilliant men who helped establish the

James Madison as he appeared in his last years.

Dolley Madison moved back to Washington after her husband's death and even served as the hostess for parties in the White House during the presidency of Martin Van Buren.

United States. Madison, the youngest of the group, is less familiar and deserves more credit than he often receives.

Madison had the special ability to build a bridge between the ideals of a republican government and the often messy workings of a government in practice. He was a major architect of the nation's Constitution, helping create a document that clearly states the nation's unchanging principles but is flexible enough to meet changing conditions. The Constitution has worked so well that more than

Madison's greatest memorial is the United States Constitution, of which he was chief architect.

200 years later it is still in force. Its design has also influenced the design of dozens of new governments in countries around the world.

Madison was also one of the first political professionals. He was a master at drafting articles, letters, and speeches, often for others, including George Washington and Thomas Jefferson. Later, working with Jefferson, he was the main organizer of the Democratic-Republican party. He managed party members in Congress, directed Jefferson's political campaigns for president, and served as Jefferson's closest political adviser for eight years.

Madison's contributions as president are more difficult to judge. Lacking the huge reputation of Washington or Jefferson, unable to gain control of the Congress or of his own party, and becoming the first wartime president, Madison endured six difficult years. In his last two years, he worked to adapt the ideals of the Democratic-Republican party to new circumstances in a rapidly growing and changing country. Even if he was not always effective, most Americans would have agreed that they were better off at the end of his presidency than they had been at the beginning.

Fast Facts James Madison

Birth:	March 16, 1751
Birthplace:	Port Conway, Virginia
Parents:	James Madison, Sr., and Nelly Conway Madison
Brothers/Sisters:	Francis (1753–1800)
	Ambrose (1753–1793)
	Nelly Conway (1760–1802)
	William (1762–1843)
	Sarah Catlett (1764–1843)
	Francis Taylor (1774–1823)
	(and five others who died in infancy or childhood)
Education:	College of New Jersey (now Princeton University), graduated 1771
Occupation:	Lawyer
Marriage:	To Dolley Payne Todd Madison, September 15, 1794
Children:	None (one stepson, *see* Dolley Madison at right)
Political Party:	Democratic-Republican
Political Offices:	1776 Delegate to Virginia Constitutional Convention
	Member, Virginia General Assembly
	1777 Member, Virginia Council of State
	1780 Delegate to the Continental Congress
	1783 Member, Virginia General Assembly
	1787 Delegate to the Constitutional Convention
	1789–1797 Congressman, U.S. House of Representatives
	1801–1809 Secretary of state under President Thomas Jefferson
	1809–1817 President of the United States
His Vice Presidents:	1809–1812 George Clinton (died in office)
	1813–1814 Elbridge Gerry (died in office)
Major Policy Decisions as President:	1811 Refused to renew the charter of the Bank of the United States
	1812 Requested that Congress declare war on Great Britain, served as first wartime president
Firsts:	First president who had served in Congress
	First president to issue a war proclamation against a foreign nation
Death:	June 28, 1836
Age at Death:	85 years
Burial Place:	Montpelier (family estate), Orange County, Virginia

Fast Facts Dolley Payne Todd Madison

Birth:	May 20, 1768
Birthplace:	Guilford County, North Carolina
Parents:	John Payne and Mary Coles Payne
Brothers/Sisters:	Four brothers: Walter, William Temple, Isaac, and John
	Three sisters: Lucy, Anna, and Mary
Education:	Home taught
Marriages:	Married John Todd Jr., 1792 (he died 1793)
	Married James Madison, September 15, 1794
Children:	John Payne Todd (1792–1853), known as Payne Todd
	William Temple Todd (1793–1793)
Firsts:	First ever to send a personal message by telegram (1844)
Death:	July 12, 1849
Age at Death:	81 years
Burial Place:	Montpelier (Madison family estate), Orange County, Virginia

Timeline

1751	1771	1775	1776	1777
Born in Port Conway, Virginia, on March 16. 	Graduates from the College of New Jersey (Princeton University today) and returns to the family estate, Montpelier, in Virginia.	American Revolution begins; Madison is appointed a colonel in the Orange County militia.	Becomes a delegate to the Virginia Constitutional Convention; is elected to the new General Assembly.	Appointed to the Virginia Council of State, which advised the governor.

1789	1792	1794	1797	1799
Elected to the House of Representatives.	Becomes a founder and leader of the Democratic-Republican party.	Courts and marries Dolley Payne Todd.	Leaves Congress and returns to Montpelier.	Elected to the Virginia state legislature.

1814 (Sept.)	1814 (Dec.)	1815 (Jan.)	1817	1836
British troops capture Washington, D.C., and burn government buildings.	British and Americans agree to Treaty of Ghent, which restores pre-war borders.	Americans defeat British outside New Orleans before news of the treaty arrives.	Retires to Montpelier; his secretary of state James Monroe becomes president.	Dies at Montpelier on June 28 at the age of 85.

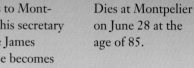

1780	1783	1785	1787	1787–88
Becomes a delegate to the Continental Congress in Philadelphia.	Leaves Congress and returns to the Virginia assembly.	Helps to pass a Virginia statute promising religious freedom.	Represents Virginia at the Constitutional Convention and takes a leading role in shaping the new Constitution.	Campaigns for ratification of the Constitution.

1801	1809	1811	1812	1813
Appointed secretary of state and becomes President Thomas Jefferson's closest adviser.	Succeeds Jefferson and becomes the fourth president of the United States.	Relations with the British worsen.	United States declares war on Great Britain.	Begins second term. Americans defeat British in the Battle of Lake Erie and at the Thames River (Canada).

Glossary

anarchy: complete disorder and lawlessness

aristocracy: a class of people who control most of the wealth and power in a society

bill of rights: part of a legal document that lists the essential rights of individuals

boycott: a state's or region's decision not to buy goods from another state or region

democracy: a form of government in which the mass of people rule themselves directly or through elected representatives

duties: taxes on goods coming into a state or country from another state or country

embargo: a law or decree that prohibits trade with another state or country

executive: the part of a government responsible for seeing that the laws are followed or executed; the head of the executive is often a single person such as the president.

federal government: in the United States, the national government based in Washington, D.C. The U.S. Constitution and later court decisions outline its responsibilities and powers.

impress: to force a person to serve in a military organization against his or her consent

judiciary: the part of a government that interprets the laws when there are disagreements; these questions are settled by judges.

legislature: the part of a government that passes laws or legislates; in a democracy, the legislature is a group of representatives elected by people of different regions; in the United States, the legislature is called the Congress.

ratify: to approve a legal document (such as the U.S. Constitution) and put it into effect

veto: rejection of a bill (a proposed law) by the executive

Further Reading

Gaines, Anne Graham. *James Madison: Our Fourth President*. Chanhassen, MN: Child's World, 2002.

Malone, Mary. *James Madison*. Springfield, NJ: Enslow Publishers, 1997.

Santella, Andrew. *James Madison*. Minneapolis, MN: Compass Point Books, 2002.

MORE ADVANCED READING

Ellis, Joseph J. *Founding Brothers: The Revolutionary Generation*. New York: Alfred A. Knopf, 2000.

Ketcham, Ralph. *James Madison, A Biography*. New York: Macmillan, 1971.

McCoy, Drew R. *The Last of the Fathers: James Madison and the Republican Legacy*. New York: Cambridge University Press, 1989.

Rakove, Jack N. *James Madison and the Creation of the American Republic*. New York: Longman, 2002.

Stagg, J. C. *Mr. Madison's War: Politics, Diplomacy, and Warfare in the Early American Republic*. Princeton, NJ: Princeton University Press, 1983.

Wills, Gary. *James Madison*. New York: Times Books, 2002.

Places to Visit

★ ★ ★ ★ ★

Montpelier

Madison's plantation, in Orange County, Virginia, northeast of Charlottesville, is open to the public seven days a week.

P.O. Box 911
Orange, VA 22960
(540) 672-2728

The James Madison Museum

A small museum in the town of Orange, near Montpelier.

129 Caroline Street
Orange, VA 22960-1532
(540) 672-1776

Independence Hall

Once called the Old Statehouse, Independence Hall in Philadelphia is the site where the Declaration of Independence was signed in 1776 and where Madison attended the Constitutional Convention in 1787. Now a National Historic Site operated by the National Park Service, it receives nearly 3 million visitors a year.

143 South Third Street
Philadelphia, PA 19106
(215) 597-8974

Online Sites of Interest

★ **The White House**

http://www.whitehouse.gov/history/presidents/jm4.html

This link provides a brief biography of Madison. The White House site also includes many details about the presidential residence from 1800 to the present; information on first ladies, including Dolley Madison; and activities for kids.

★ **Internet Public Library, Presidents of the United States (POTUS)**

http:/www.ipl.si.umich.edu/div/potus/jmadison.html

A good resource for information on Madison. It includes links to many other sites with more information.

★ **The American President**

www.americanpresident.org

Provides a brief biography and offers greater detail on many aspects of each president's life and the times he lived in.

★ **James Madison's Montpelier**

http://www.montpelier.org

A site that describes James Madison's estate in Orange County, Virginia, and his life there. *See also* "Places to Visit."

★ **James Madison University**

http://www.jmu.edu/madison/

This excellent site offers much information on Madison as a man and as a political leader.

★ **The James Madison Papers**

http://www.virginia.edu/pjm/

Provides a brief biography and information on the project to edit and publish Madison's papers in a modern edition.

★ **The Dolley Madison Project**

http://moderntimes.vcdh.virginia.edu/madison/

A charming and informative site about Dolley Madison's life and times. It points out that she knew every one of the first twelve presidents.

Table of Presidents

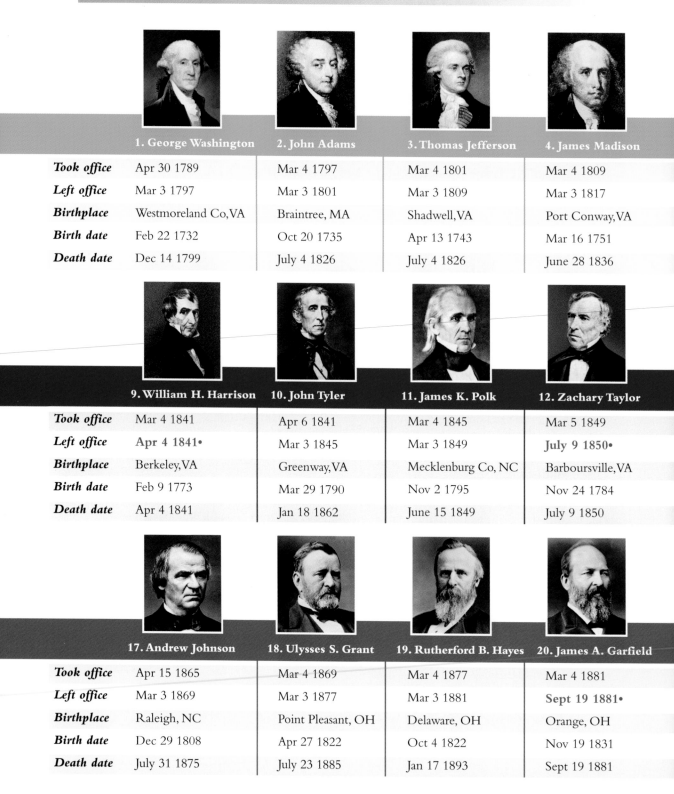

	1. George Washington	**2. John Adams**	**3. Thomas Jefferson**	**4. James Madison**
Took office	Apr 30 1789	Mar 4 1797	Mar 4 1801	Mar 4 1809
Left office	Mar 3 1797	Mar 3 1801	Mar 3 1809	Mar 3 1817
Birthplace	Westmoreland Co, VA	Braintree, MA	Shadwell, VA	Port Conway, VA
Birth date	Feb 22 1732	Oct 20 1735	Apr 13 1743	Mar 16 1751
Death date	Dec 14 1799	July 4 1826	July 4 1826	June 28 1836

	9. William H. Harrison	**10. John Tyler**	**11. James K. Polk**	**12. Zachary Taylor**
Took office	Mar 4 1841	Apr 6 1841	Mar 4 1845	Mar 5 1849
Left office	Apr 4 1841•	Mar 3 1845	Mar 3 1849	July 9 1850•
Birthplace	Berkeley, VA	Greenway, VA	Mecklenburg Co, NC	Barboursville, VA
Birth date	Feb 9 1773	Mar 29 1790	Nov 2 1795	Nov 24 1784
Death date	Apr 4 1841	Jan 18 1862	June 15 1849	July 9 1850

	17. Andrew Johnson	**18. Ulysses S. Grant**	**19. Rutherford B. Hayes**	**20. James A. Garfield**
Took office	Apr 15 1865	Mar 4 1869	Mar 4 1877	Mar 4 1881
Left office	Mar 3 1869	Mar 3 1877	Mar 3 1881	Sept 19 1881•
Birthplace	Raleigh, NC	Point Pleasant, OH	Delaware, OH	Orange, OH
Birth date	Dec 29 1808	Apr 27 1822	Oct 4 1822	Nov 19 1831
Death date	July 31 1875	July 23 1885	Jan 17 1893	Sept 19 1881

	5. James Monroe	6. John Quincy Adams	7. Andrew Jackson	8. Martin Van Buren
	Mar 4 1817	Mar 4 1825	Mar 4 1829	Mar 4 1837
	Mar 3 1825	Mar 3 1829	Mar 3 1837	Mar 3 1841
	Westmoreland Co, VA	Braintree, MA	The Waxhaws, SC	Kinderhook, NY
	Apr 28 1758	July 11 1767	Mar 15 1767	Dec 5 1782
	July 4 1831	Feb 23 1848	June 8 1845	July 24 1862

	13. Millard Fillmore	14. Franklin Pierce	15. James Buchanan	16. Abraham Lincoln
	July 9 1850	Mar 4 1853	Mar 4 1857	Mar 4 1861
	Mar 3 1853	Mar 3 1857	Mar 3 1861	Apr 15 1865•
	Locke Township, NY	Hillsborough, NH	Cove Gap, PA	Hardin Co, KY
	Jan 7 1800	Nov 23 1804	Apr 23 1791	Feb 12 1809
	Mar 8 1874	Oct 8 1869	June 1 1868	Apr 15 1865

	21. Chester A. Arthur	22. Grover Cleveland	23. Benjamin Harrison	24. Grover Cleveland
	Sept 19 1881	Mar 4 1885	Mar 4 1889	Mar 4 1893
	Mar 3 1885	Mar 3 1889	Mar 3 1893	Mar 3 1897
	Fairfield, VT	Caldwell, NJ	North Bend, OH	Caldwell, NJ
	Oct 5 1830	Mar 18 1837	Aug 20 1833	Mar 18 1837
	Nov 18 1886	June 24 1908	Mar 13 1901	June 24 1908

	25. William McKinley	26. Theodore Roosevelt	27. William H. Taft	28. Woodrow Wilson
Took office	Mar 4 1897	Sept 14 1901	Mar 4 1909	Mar 4 1913
Left office	Sept 14 1901•	Mar 3 1909	Mar 3 1913	Mar 3 1921
Birthplace	Niles, OH	New York, NY	Cincinnati, OH	Staunton, VA
Birth date	Jan 29 1843	Oct 27 1858	Sept 15 1857	Dec 28 1856
Death date	Sept 14 1901	Jan 6 1919	Mar 8 1930	Feb 3 1924

	33. Harry S. Truman	34. Dwight D. Eisenhower	35. John F. Kennedy	36. Lyndon B. Johnson
Took office	Apr 12 1945	Jan 20 1953	Jan 20 1961	Nov 22 1963
Left office	Jan 20 1953	Jan 20 1961	Nov 22 1963•	Jan 20 1969
Birthplace	Lamar, MO	Denison, TX	Brookline, MA	Johnson City, TX
Birth date	May 8 1884	Oct 14 1890	May 29 1917	Aug 27 1908
Death date	Dec 26 1972	Mar 28 1969	Nov 22 1963	Jan 22 1973

	41. George Bush	42. Bill Clinton	43. George W. Bush
Took office	Jan 20 1989	Jan 20 1993	Jan 20 2001
Left office	Jan 20 1993	Jan 20 2001	—
Birthplace	Milton, MA	Hope, AR	New Haven, CT
Birth date	June 12 1924	Aug 19 1946	July 6 1946
Death date	—	—	—

29. Warren G. Harding	30. Calvin Coolidge	31. Herbert Hoover	32. Franklin D. Roosevelt
Mar 4 1921	Aug 2 1923	Mar 4 1929	Mar 4 1933
Aug 2 1923•	Mar 3 1929	Mar 3 1933	**Apr 12 1945•**
Blooming Grove, OH	Plymouth, VT	West Branch, IA	Hyde Park, NY
Nov 21 1865	July 4 1872	Aug 10 1874	Jan 30 1882
Aug 2 1923	Jan 5 1933	Oct 20 1964	Apr 12 1945

37. Richard M. Nixon	38. Gerald R. Ford	39. Jimmy Carter	40. Ronald Reagan
Jan 20 1969	Aug 9 1974	Jan 20 1977	Jan 20 1981
Aug 9 1974★	Jan 20 1977	Jan 20 1981	Jan 20 1989
Yorba Linda, CA	Omaha, NE	Plains, GA	Tampico, IL
Jan 9 1913	July 14 1913	Oct 1 1924	Feb 11 1911
Apr 22 1994	—	—	

• Indicates the president died while in office.

★ Richard Nixon resigned before his term expired.

Index

About the Author

Brendan January is an award winning author of more than twenty nonfiction books for children. January is a graduate of the Columbia Graduate School of Journalism and a Fulbright Scholar. He lives in Jersey City, New Jersey, with his wife.